Hiking Women

A
WANDERER'S
JOURNAL

Hiking Women

A
WANDERER'S
JOURNAL

GUIDED PROMPTS
for Solo Female Explorers

JENNIFER DOEHRING

Countryman Press

An Imprint of W. W. Norton & Company
Independent Publishers Since 1923

HIKING WOMEN is a journal template for hikers to use to record their thoughts and experiences on and off the trail. While this book includes a few fun facts and informational illustrations, it is not an instructional text, a technical hiking manual, nor a comprehensive hiking guide. Before embarking on a hike of any duration, the reader is advised to consult sources specifically written to educate hikers about hiking conditions and hazards, appropriate hiking and camping clothing and gear, choosing hiking routes, hiking permits and trail etiquette, setting up camp, and how to handle difficult circumstances on the trail or while camping.

For information about permission to reproduce selections from this book, write to Permissions, Countryman Press, 500 Fifth Avenue, New York, NY 10110

For information about special discounts for bulk purchases, please contact W. W. Norton Special Sales at specialsales@wwnorton.com or 800-233-4830

Manufacturing through Imago
Book design by Allison Chi
Production manager: Devon Zahn

Countryman Press
www.countrymanpress.com

An imprint of W. W. Norton & Company, Inc.
500 Fifth Avenue, New York, NY 10110
www.wwnorton.com

978-1-68268-906-6

10 9 8 7 6 5 4 3 2 1

To Jeff, for inspiring strength on my long solo hikes.

How to Use this Book

While you're out in nature, think of this journal as a friendly companion. Something to turn to in quiet moments, in your tent at night, or at any time after your trip. It's intended to help you to remember the small yet magical details, record growth and reflection, and appreciate and keep track of every hike—short or long. Some prompts are silly, some are practical, and many are contemplative—perfect for the alone time you'll have.

This book has no set order, so please jump around! Pick and choose your way through the book, stopping to answer whatever compels you in the moment.

You'll notice that some prompt pages are meant to be an answer-once prompt (though it's your journal—use it anyway you want!), while others are good for a number of different hikes.

To keep track of each hike's entries, there are index pages where in addition to recording where you hiked, what trail(s) you were on, the weather, etc., you can indicate which pages in the journal you filled out.

HIKE INDEX

Date___3/6/23___ Place_Arches National Park_____

Distance___6.7 mi___ Duration_Day hike___ Conditions_Snowy!___

Backpack ❑ Day Pack ☒ No Pack ❑

Prompt Pages Used_4,36,44,110,115_____

Extra Notes_March in the desert, I wouldn't even think about_
the chances of snow, but we happened to arrive right
after a snowfall! It was beautiful.

Later, when the book is full, it serves as a memory keeper of hikes, triumphs, thoughts, beauty, and things you saw, felt, and did along the way.

So what are you waiting for? Get out there and explore! You've got this!

Jot down some names/numbers here in case of emergency.

Before and While Heading Off Solo

- Let others know where you're going and when you expect to return.

- Be overprepared. Take more water than you need and pack a water filter so you can safely collect water in emergencies.

- Carry bear spray or pepper spray just in case.

- Be vigilant. Know who and what is around you.

- It is better to not wear headphones so you can listen to your surroundings.

- Check the trail conditions beforehand.

- Always have a hike-appropriate first-aid kit in your pack.

- Pack sandals in case you need to cross a river or stretch of water. Keep your boots/socks dry at all costs!

- Many hikers have gotten lost or hurt less than a mile from the trail. Stay on the trail at all times for safety.

What are some rules you've given yourself when you're out hiking alone?

RULES

-
-
-
-
-
-
-

When you researched this hike, what drew you to it the most? View? Traffic? Landscape features? Wildlife? Elevation?

Date:

Date:

Date:

Date:

Date:

Date:

What's in your backpack for this hike?

Essentials:

Oddities:

Comfort:

Wish I had:

Essentials:

Oddities:

Comfort:

Wish I had:

My Dream Hike

My dream hike would be set in the middle of _____

_____ during _____. On this hike, I would

have my favorite _____, which always makes for _____

_____.

It's _____ this time of year, so I make sure to _____

_____ and _____

_____.

Once everything is packed, I set out on the trail, which is _____

_____.

I'm so excited for _____, because _____

_____ and _____. During

my break, I pick a perfect spot to stop. It's _____and I hear

sounds of _____.

It smells like _____, which reminds me of _____

_____, and that brings me joy.

When I arrive at my destination, I'm overwhelmed with feelings of _____

_____.

I take a picture of _____ before I head back home.

Why did you start hiking?

Why do you hike now?

What are some of your favorite moments from this hike that you will remember for years to come?

Date:

Date:

Date:

Date:

Date:

Date:

There's something peaceful about being able to settle into your thoughts when you're alone. **What did you think about on the trail today?**

Who did you think about on the trail today?

What *didn't* you think about on the trail today?

Who *didn't* you think about on the trail today?

Three Basic Knots

SQUARE KNOT: A very secure, basic knot that is easy to untie (like a shoelace knot). It should not be used to hold anything heavy.

THIEF KNOT: Similar to a square knot, but the ends are opposite to each other. Sailors invented this as a tell-tale sign: if someone rifled their sea bag, chances are the thief would retie the bag with a square knot.

BOWLINE KNOT: Creates a fixed loop at the end of a rope. This type of knot is best used if there is constant pressure pulling against the knot.

Think back to your first solo hike. In what ways was it different than you expected? **Use this box to capture the positive feelings you had the first time you hiked by yourself.**

Hiking alone can be empowering. **In what ways has your confidence been boosted through this hike?**

Date:

Date:

Date:

Date:

Date:

Date:

What's the longest you've been alone? Like really, truly alone?

Remember to take time to sit with your thoughts. **What have you discovered about yourself through that "aloneness"?**

Solitude is a great teacher. **If you could go back in time right now, what are five things you would tell your younger self?**

Notes, Ideas, and Reflections

The longest-living fern species
can live to be 100 years old.

"All truly great thoughts are conceived while walking."
—FRIEDRICH NIETZSCHE

Walking gets the brain flowing. **Write down some creative thoughts and ideas you've had since starting this hike.**

When you pass another hiker on the trail:

What did you say?

What should you have said?

Things you'll remember to say next time?

What did you say?

What should you have said?

Things you'll remember to say next time?

If you could name the trail you are/were hiking today, what would you call it? Remember to include the date!

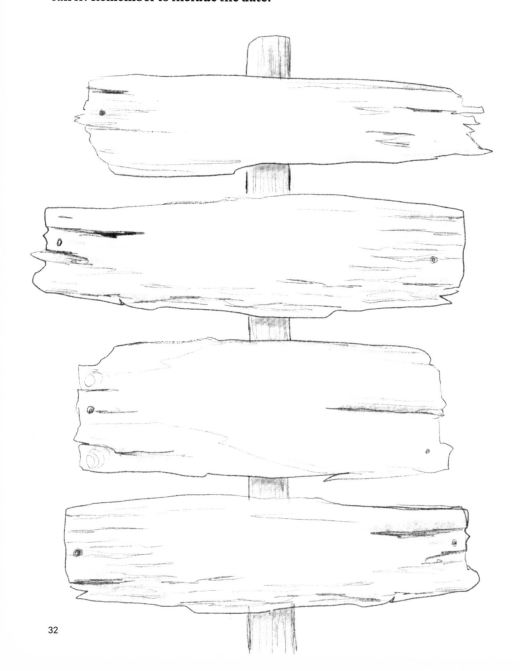

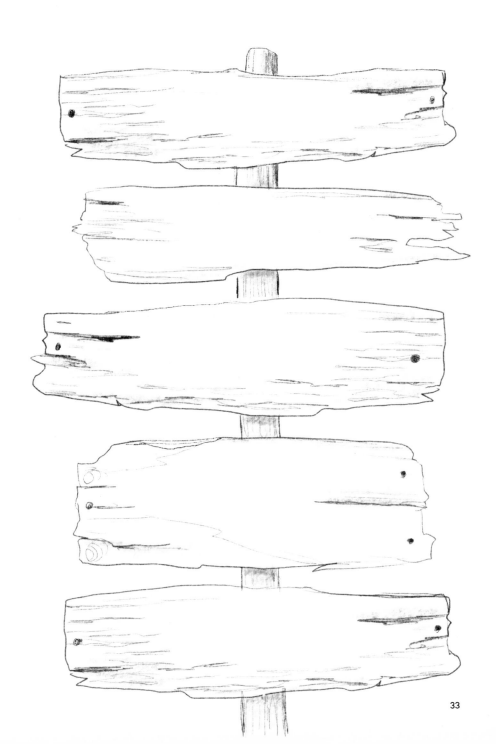

It's a myth that mosquitoes bite women more frequently than men. Mosquitoes are drawn to body heat and carbon dioxide, so men statistically are bitten more often. **What were you bitten or stung by on this hike?**

Date:	Date:
Date:	**Date:**

Common Wisdom for Most Insect Bites and Stings
- Remove the stinger or hairs if still in the skin.
- Take an over-the-counter antihistamine to help with allergic reactions.
- Carry pain-relieving cream in case of a bite or sting.
- Watch for severe symptoms: impaired speech, muscle spasms, vomiting, etc.

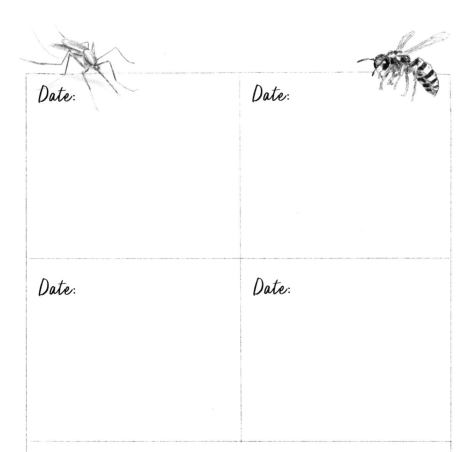

Date:

Date:

Date:

Date:

- Wash the infected area with soap and water, if possible, and then apply an antibiotic ointment.
- Use a cold compress to reduce swelling and pain.
- Try not to scratch or itch the area, as it can become infected.
- If the bite or sting is on an arm or leg, keep the area elevated to help reduce swelling.

Desert Land Formations

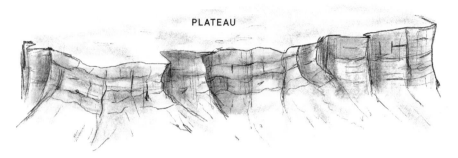

PLATEAU

Plateaus, sometimes called tablelands, are flat-topped areas rising sharply above the land below on one or more sides, while other sides may slope or ease into the landscape. The largest in North America is the Colorado Plateau (130,000 square miles), which overlaps corners of Colorado, Utah, Arizona, and New Mexico and contains eight national parks.

Mesas, formed by erosion, are tall, visibly layered land masses with flat tops and steep sides all around that stand above the landscape. Mesas are typically isolated on the landscape and are wider than they are tall.

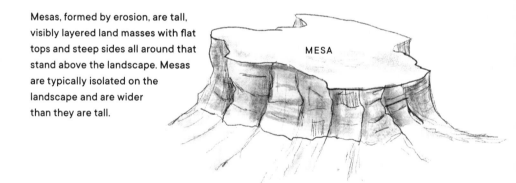

MESA

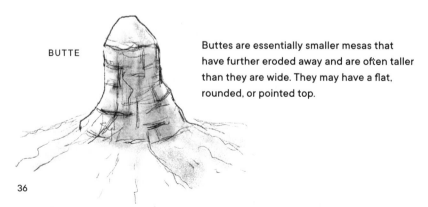

BUTTE

Buttes are essentially smaller mesas that have further eroded away and are often taller than they are wide. They may have a flat, rounded, or pointed top.

What land formations did you see on your hike today?

Date:

Date:

Date:

Date:

Desert vs. Forest

What is your forest dream trail and why?

What time of year you would hike?

What you'd most look forward to seeing?

What you'd wear?

What you'd bring?

What is your desert dream trail and why?

What time of year you would hike?

What you'd most look forward to seeing?

What you'd wear?

What you'd bring?

Would you rather:
Set up camp in the snow or sand?

Take a camping trip through the west coast or the east coast?

Hike a long flat trail or a short steep one?

Have a run in with wasps or mosquitoes?

Notes, Ideas, and Reflections

Most women are taught that being alone is unsafe. From an early age, we are encouraged to travel in groups and stay in well-lit and well-trafficked places, to see ourselves as perpetually vulnerable. **In what ways are you fierce, capable, and strong?**

Things men don't have to think about on the trail that you do:

What scares you the most about hiking alone? Don't overthink! **Quickly jot down some words in the box below. Then draw a bigger box around it to contain them all.** Fear is healthy and even useful, provided it is kept in check.

Do you have a mantra in your head when you hike? If so, what is it?

If not, use this space to try some out.

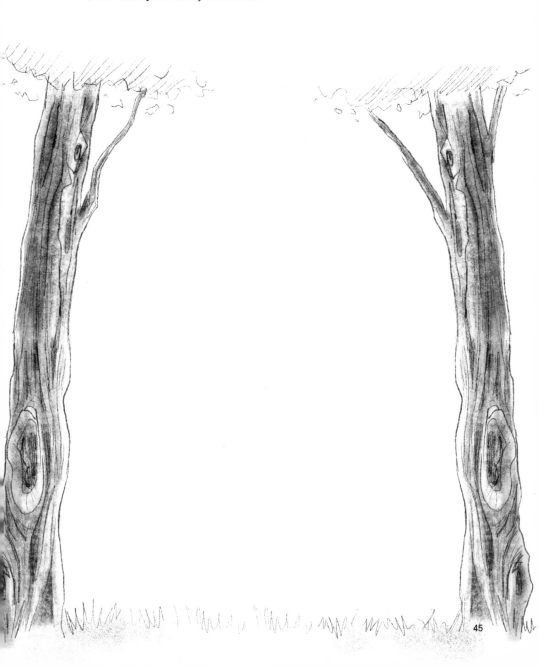

Diagram Your Fears and Conquer Them!

Example

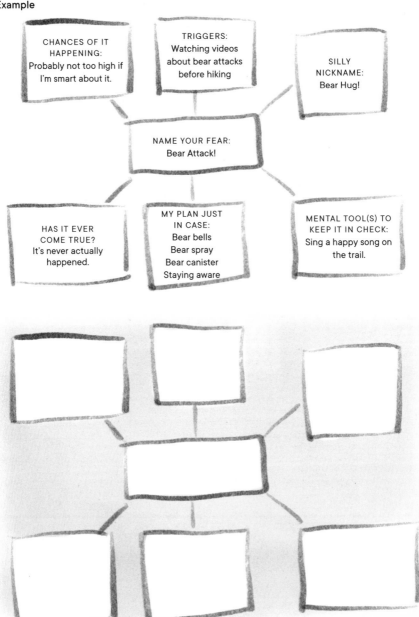

CHANCES OF IT HAPPENING:
Probably not too high if I'm smart about it.

TRIGGERS:
Watching videos about bear attacks before hiking

SILLY NICKNAME:
Bear Hug!

NAME YOUR FEAR:
Bear Attack!

HAS IT EVER COME TRUE?
It's never actually happened.

MY PLAN JUST IN CASE:
Bear bells
Bear spray
Bear canister
Staying aware

MENTAL TOOL(S) TO KEEP IT IN CHECK:
Sing a happy song on the trail.

Fear meter on this hike:

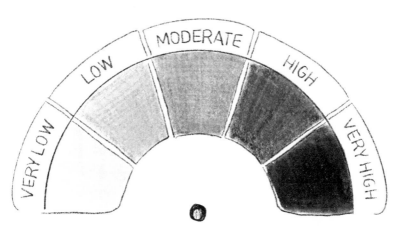

Peace meter on this hike:

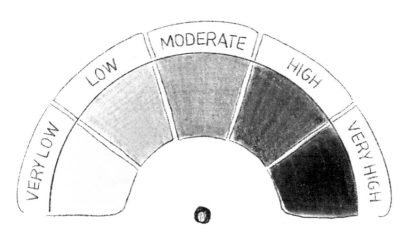

Fear meter on this hike:

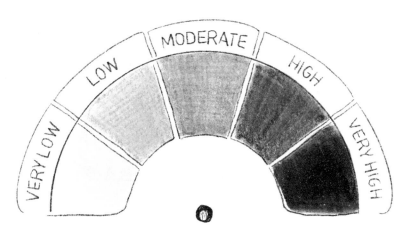

Peace meter on this hike:

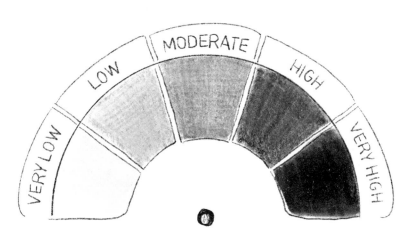

Being scared is normal; in fact, it's healthy! Don't let fear take away the beauty of this hike. **Write down some things that gave you peace today and made you forget your fear:**

Date:

Date:

Date:

At what point today did you have complete peace of mind?

Date:

Date:

Date:

Gratitude lessens anxiety, so take this moment to stop and appreciate what you're grateful for today.

Date:

Date:

Date:

Date:

Date:

Date:

Date:

Date:

"Hiking is not for everyone.
Notice the wilderness is mostly empty."
—SONJA YOERG

How far into your hike were you today before you felt fully your singular self?

Date:

Date:

Date:

Date:

What parts of your identity got left behind once you were on the trail?

Date:

Date:

Date:

Date:

Would you rather:

Hike 10 miles straight uphill or straight downhill?

Hike in the desert or the forest?

Take a four-day hike solo or with a group?

Hike in a foot of snow or in a thunderstorm?

Notes, Ideas, and Reflections

An Elevation Map of Your Day

Example

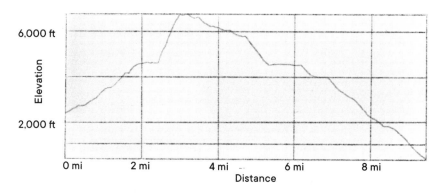

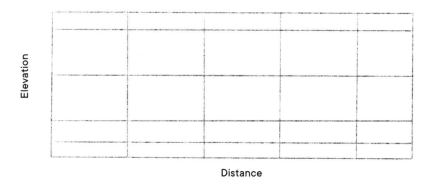

Elevation

Distance

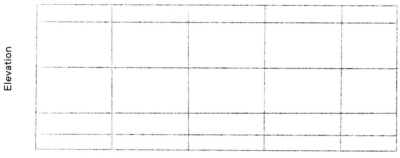

Elevation

Distance

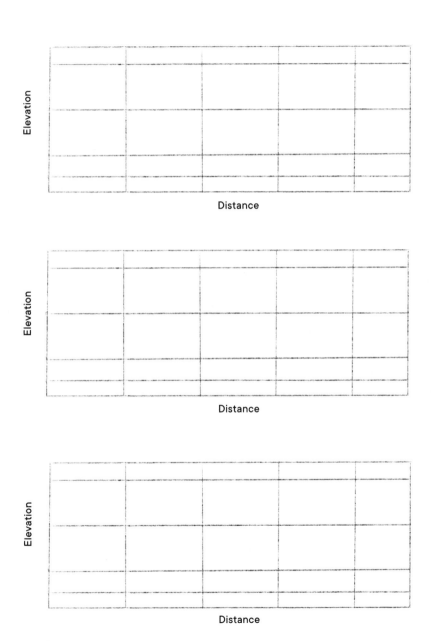

What are your bucket list trips? **Make a list here and cross them off as your future self completes them.**

What are your favorite types of trails/terrains and why? How does that change depending on the type of trip? (Backpacking, day hike, camping trip, etc.)

Which national parks have you been to?

Circle the ones you've visited!

BRYCE CANYON   CANYONLANDS   CARLSBAD CAVERNS   CAPITOL REEF   CHANNEL ISLANDS

CUYAHOGA VALLEY   DEATH VALLEY   DENALI   DRY TORTUGAS   EVERGLADES

GLACIER BAY   GLACIER   GRAND CANYON   GRAND TETON   GREAT SAND DUNES

GUADALUPE   HALEAKALA   VOLCANOES   HOT SPRINGS   INDIANA DUNES

KATMAI   KINGS CANYON   KENAI FJORDS   KOBUK VALLEY   LAKE CLARK

BISCAYNE   BLACK CANYON   CONGAREE   CRATER LAKE   GATES OF THE ARCTIC

MT RAINIER

GREAT BASIN

YELLOWSTONE

REDWOOD

ROCKY MOUNTAIN

ISLE ROYALE

JOSHUA TREE

MESA VERDE

VOYAGERS

WIND CAVE

LASSEN VOLCANIC

MAMMOTH CAVE

GATEWAY ARCH

NEW RIVER GORGE

NORTH CASCADES

OLYMPIC

PETRIFIED FOREST

PINNACLES

SAGUARO

SEQUOIA

SHENANDOAH

ROOSEVELT

VIRGIN ISLANDS

WHITE SANDS

WRANGELL ST ELIAS

GREAT SMOKEY MOUNTAINS

YOSEMITE

ZION

ACADIA

AMERICAN SAMOA

ARCHES

BADLANDS

BIG BEND

What favorite thing did you bring in your backpack today?

What's your most-used item on any one hike?

What's the most coveted item you've seen another hiker use?

Possible Uses for Duct Tape

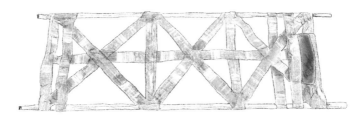

Field stretcher

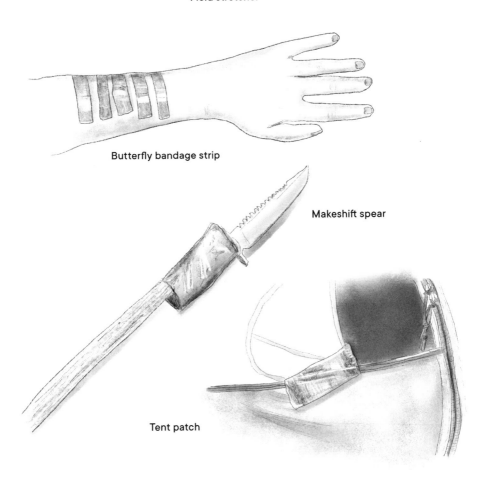

Butterfly bandage strip

Makeshift spear

Tent patch

Internal Dialogue When I'm Hiking

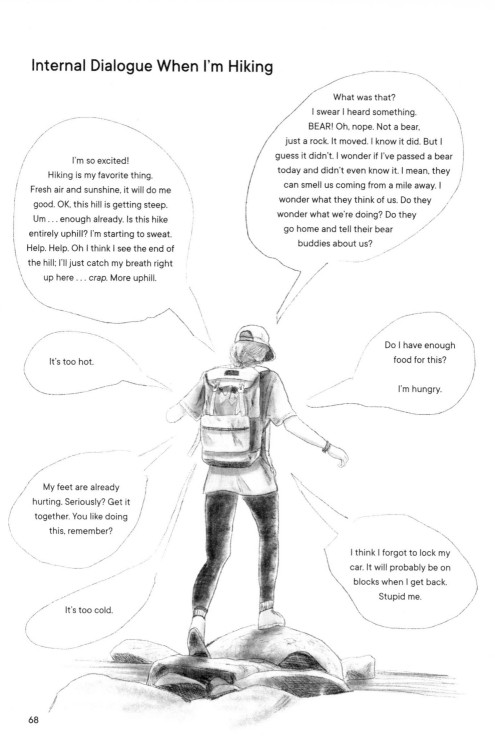

What was that? I swear I heard something. BEAR! Oh, nope. Not a bear, just a rock. It moved. I know it did. But I guess it didn't. I wonder if I've passed a bear today and didn't even know it. I mean, they can smell us coming from a mile away. I wonder what they think of us. Do they wonder what we're doing? Do they go home and tell their bear buddies about us?

I'm so excited! Hiking is my favorite thing. Fresh air and sunshine, it will do me good. OK, this hill is getting steep. Um . . . enough already. Is this hike entirely uphill? I'm starting to sweat. Help. Help. Oh I think I see the end of the hill; I'll just catch my breath right up here . . . *crap.* More uphill.

It's too hot.

Do I have enough food for this?

I'm hungry.

My feet are already hurting. Seriously? Get it together. You like doing this, remember?

It's too cold.

I think I forgot to lock my car. It will probably be on blocks when I get back. Stupid me.

What's your internal dialogue? Anything goes!

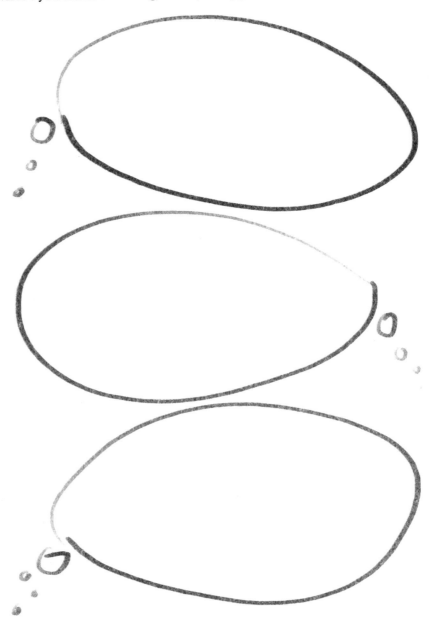

Be your own hiking coach! **What internal dialogue will keep you motivated and positive on the trail?**

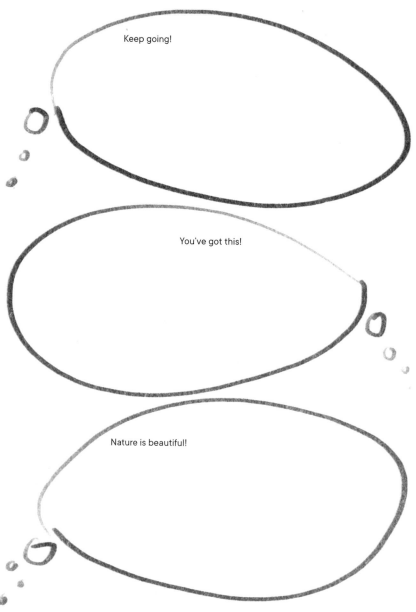

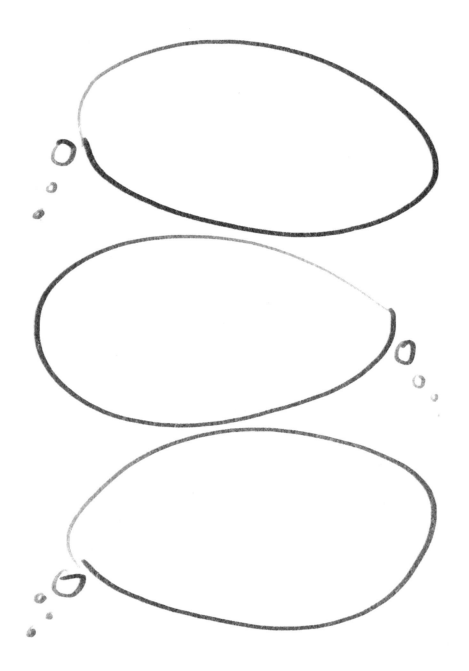

There are over 300,000 different species of flowering plants in the world. **Note which ones you see on your hikes, paying particular attention to what makes them different from one another.**

Date:

Date:

Date:

Date:

What makes you unique and different compared to your friends and family, and why is that a good thing?

"There is no limit to what we, as women, can accomplish."
—MICHELLE OBAMA

What other women did you encounter today? Make up a reason you think they hike. Give them trail names, too.

Best things about hiking alone?

Worst things about hiking alone?

When has being alone been most exhilarating on this hike? What moments did you wish you could have turned to someone?

Date:

Date:

Date:

Date:

Date:

Date:

Imagine someone was here with you on this hike. **Who would you want it to be and why?**

Write a personal-style ad as if you were seeking a hiking partner:

About me: _____

_____

_____

Seeking: _____

_____

_____

Must: _____

_____

_____

Must Not: _____

_____

_____

Bonus Points: _____

_____

_____

"You're always with yourself,
so you might as well enjoy the company."
—DIANE VON FÜRSTENBERG

What is this hike specifically a break from?

Date:

Date:

Date:

Date:

Date:

Date:

Describe the color palette of your favorite spot on your hike today. Give the colors paint-like or Crayola-like names in your description.

Tinder Sources in Nature

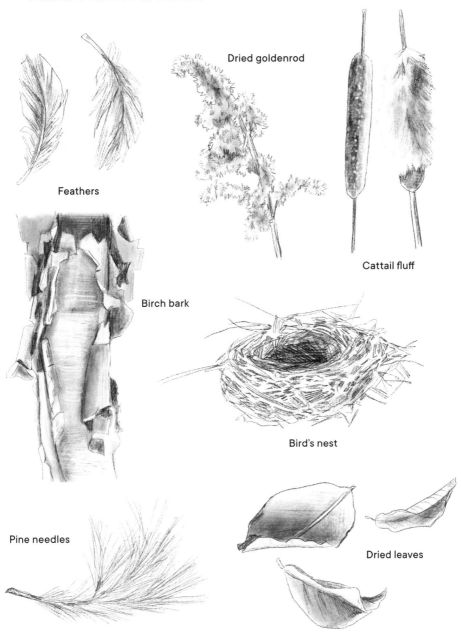

Feathers

Dried goldenrod

Cattail fluff

Birch bark

Bird's nest

Pine needles

Dried leaves

Overnight on the trail! **How is your sleep different than when you're at home?**

Did you have any dreams?

Did you have any clear thoughts that wouldn't have been possible back at home?

What do you do to make your campsite yours? What do you think you do the same as most hikers, and what do you do that's unique?

Take a moment to make friends with your surroundings. **Draw or list what's around your campsite (rocks, plants, trees, etc.) and give them names.** Let them be your friends for the night.

What makes you feel safe or secure in your tent at night when you're alone? What do you do to calm your mind?

What's for breakfast? What are you having vs. what you wish you were having? Extra points if it's the same thing!

Having:

Wish I was having:

Write down the first things you heard/saw/smelled/did when you came out of your tent.

Dream Campsite

My dream campsite is set up next to _____ in a

_____. After a satisfying meal of _____

_____, I fall asleep to the sound of _____.

I wake up in the morning with _____ and I step out of my

tent. I immediately hear _____. This is very exciting

because _____.

I fish in my backpack for _____, _____

and of course I can't forget the _____.

I will always remember this trip because _____

_____

_____

_____.

94

Trail food can get monotonous. **What foods are you dreaming about having once you're finished hiking?**

Walking can grind the gears a bit too much sometimes! Switch it up. **Give yourself 10 minutes to move in a different way. Stretch, do some yoga, or meditate. Make a note of what works best and provides needed relief.**

We feel every good hike in our body. **Take a moment to circle or capture where you hurt or ache the most after a hike.** Pay attention to patterns over time—there may be solutions, fixes, or adjustments to be made!

Date:

Date:

Date:

Date:

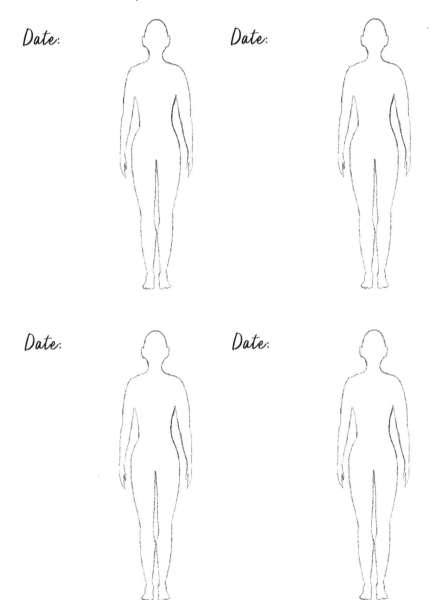

Constant hiking can really take a toll on your feet! **Take note of where your blisters and raw spots are.** They are badges of a good hike; but if they are in the same spots consistently, you might need to check your footwear.

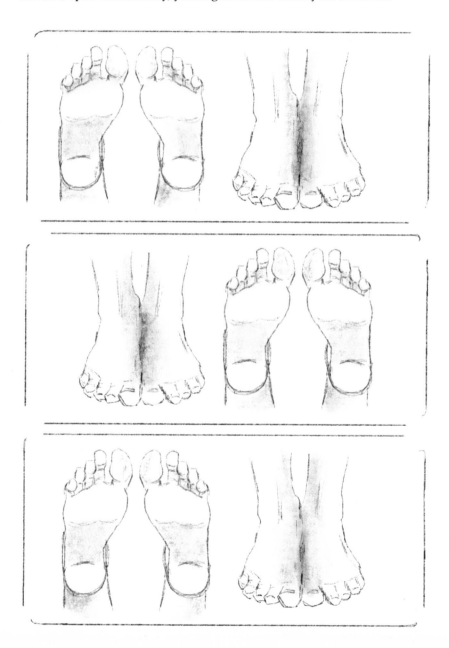

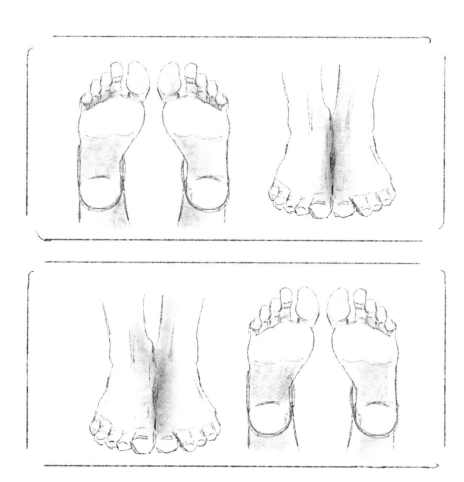

Common Wisdom for Most Blisters and Raw Spots

First, clean the blister as best you can. Then, use an antibiotic ointment to make sure the area doesn't become infected, and cover with a bandage. If you are continuing to hike, for added protection and to prevent further irritation, use moleskin or add an extra layer of gauze and tape to the top.

As a female hiker, how do you feel out in nature compared to being at work or with family? What shifts?

There's nothing like the energy of women supporting women! **Plan the perfect hiking or camping trip you'd want to take with a particular female friend.**

Location:

Time of year:

What to bring:

When you're not on the trail, pretend that you are and have lost your way. **Write down the following helpful things you can turn to on a future hike if you find yourself lost.** First, keep calm and levelheaded. **What are your tools for talking yourself out of a panic?**

What do you have in your pack that will help you find your way?

What do you have that will help you stay safe until morning, if it comes to that?

Who knows your itinerary well and will look for you if you don't check in?

How to *Not* Walk in Circles if You're Lost in the Woods

1. Choose three trees roughly in a line toward the direction you want to go.

2. When you get to the middle tree, look at the third tree and pick two more after that, for a new set of three.

3. Repeat.

Map Advice

Tip 1. If you're not packing detailed paper maps, be sure to download the maps you want—and the larger surrounding area—directly onto your smart phone. That way you can access them when you are without a cell signal or Wi-Fi.

Tip 2. Before you leave, download an app that will pull your coordinates from your phone's GPS location finder without you having a cell signal or Wi-Fi.

Tip 3. For paper maps, be sure to check the map orientation. Most maps feature a "compass rose" in one corner that shows which directions are indicated by various markers. Unless otherwise speci-fied, the top will always correspond with north.

Tip 4. Pay attention to scale. A map's scale provides a ratio of map distance to actual distance, and this can vary from map to map. Hint: Hiking maps usually have a scale of 1:25,000.

The John Muir Trail

What do you keep on you/pack with you to feel safer?

Have you ever needed it?

What didn't you have that would have come in handy?

Notes, Ideas, and Reflections

Always dress for the conditions! **For a warm-weather hike, the best outfit for me would be:**

Head gear:

Outfit:

Footwear:

For colder hiking conditions, the best outfit for me would be:

Head gear:

Outfit:

Footwear:

We cry for many reasons: grief, sadness, nostalgia, anger, frustration, fear, joy, beauty, or overwhelming happiness. Even being happily alone can trigger tears of release. **What triggered some recent tears?**

Cloud Types and What They Mean

These clouds are flat on the bottom and top, though not even. They grow vertically very quickly and can be mottled-looking. This cloud indicates that rain, thunder, or worse are coming.

Altocumulus

These clouds are much smaller and cover the sky in a thin blanket-like layer. If these clouds appear in the morning, usually rain is coming in the afternoon.

Cumulonimbus

Cumulus

These clouds look like puffy, soft cotton balls, with plenty of sky separating them from one another. As long as they don't grow in mass or height, they are good clouds for hikers to see.

Stop and rest when you are tired, not exhausted. You'll make more progress that way and be kinder to your body. **What are some of the signs your body gives you when you're starting to get tired?**

Being alone dredges up all sorts of feelings. **What are the dominant feelings you've had on this hike? Are they typical?**

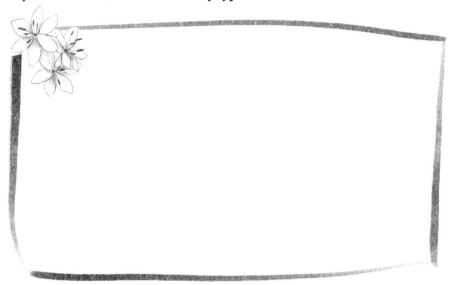

What insights did they spur?

Think back to how you felt before you left for your hike. **Now that you've completed it, how do you feel? What has shifted in your physical self?**

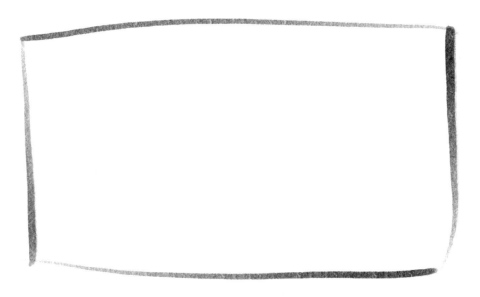

How about your mental self?

Resilience is a powerful tool. **What are some ways you've learned to turn a bad situation into something positive that helps you thrive?**

One of the world's longest-living trees is a species of bristlecone pine (*pinus longaeva*), found in Utah, Nevada, and eastern California, where some of the trees are over 4,000 years old. These pines are famously resilient, thriving in dry, inhospitable conditions.

Trees never die of old age, but rather from environmental or human factors. **What harmful factors or bad habits can you start eliminating from your own life?**

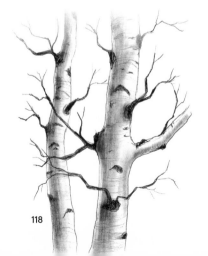

You were here. **Make a little assemblage of things you find on the ground—a mandala, a shrine, a pattern, something to say *I was here.* Just be sure to use materials that can disperse naturally. Sketch or describe it here.**

"I found far more answers in the woods than I ever did in the city."
—MARY DAVIS

Miles logged so far this year:

Goals for this year/next year:

Longest trail ever hiked:

Long distance dream hike:

HIKE INDEX

Date_____ Place_____ Hiked With_____

Distance_____ Duration_____ Conditions_____

Backpack ❏   Day Pack ❏   No Pack ❏

Prompt Pages Used_____

Extra Notes_____

_____

_____

HIKE INDEX

Date_____ Place_____ Hiked With_____

Distance_____ Duration_____ Conditions_____

Backpack ❏   Day Pack ❏   No Pack ❏

Prompt Pages Used_____

Extra Notes_____

_____

_____

HIKE INDEX

Date_____ Place_____ Hiked With_____

Distance_____ Duration_____ Conditions_____

Backpack ❏   Day Pack ❏   No Pack ❏

Prompt Pages Used_____

Extra Notes_____

_____

_____

HIKE INDEX

Date_____ Place_____ Hiked With_____

Distance_____ Duration_____ Conditions_____

Backpack ❏   Day Pack ❏   No Pack ❏

Prompt Pages Used_____

Extra Notes_____

_____

_____

HIKE INDEX

Date_____ Place_____ Hiked With_____

Distance_____ Duration_____ Conditions_____

Backpack ❏   Day Pack ❏   No Pack ❏

Prompt Pages Used_____

Extra Notes_____

_____

_____

HIKE INDEX

Date_____ Place_____ Hiked With_____

Distance_____ Duration_____ Conditions_____

Backpack ❏   Day Pack ❏   No Pack ❏

Prompt Pages Used_____

Extra Notes_____

_____

_____

HIKE INDEX

Date_____ Place_____ Hiked With_____

Distance_____ Duration_____ Conditions_____

Backpack ❏ Day Pack ❏ No Pack ❏

Prompt Pages Used_____

Extra Notes_____

_____

_____

HIKE INDEX

Date_____ Place_____ Hiked With_____

Distance_____ Duration_____ Conditions_____

Backpack ❏ Day Pack ❏ No Pack ❏

Prompt Pages Used_____

Extra Notes_____

_____

_____

HIKE INDEX

Date_____ Place_____ Hiked With_____

Distance_____ Duration_____ Conditions_____

Backpack ❏ Day Pack ❏ No Pack ❏

Prompt Pages Used_____

Extra Notes_____

_____

_____

HIKE INDEX

Date_____ Place_____ Hiked With_____

Distance_____ Duration_____ Conditions_____

Backpack ❏ Day Pack ❏ No Pack ❏

Prompt Pages Used_____

Extra Notes_____

_____

_____

HIKE INDEX

Date_____ Place_____ Hiked With_____

Distance_____ Duration_____ Conditions_____

Backpack ❏ Day Pack ❏ No Pack ❏

Prompt Pages Used_____

Extra Notes_____

_____

_____

HIKE INDEX

Date_____ Place_____ Hiked With_____

Distance_____ Duration_____ Conditions_____

Backpack ❏ Day Pack ❏ No Pack ❏

Prompt Pages Used_____

Extra Notes_____

_____

_____

HIKE INDEX

Date_____ Place_____ Hiked With_____

Distance_____ Duration_____ Conditions_____

Backpack ❏ Day Pack ❏ No Pack ❏

Prompt Pages Used_____

Extra Notes_____

_____

_____

HIKE INDEX

Date_____ Place_____ Hiked With_____

Distance_____ Duration_____ Conditions_____

Backpack ❏ Day Pack ❏ No Pack ❏

Prompt Pages Used_____

Extra Notes_____

_____

_____

HIKE INDEX

Date_____ Place_____ Hiked With_____

Distance_____ Duration_____ Conditions_____

Backpack ❏ Day Pack ❏ No Pack ❏

Prompt Pages Used_____

Extra Notes_____

_____

_____

HIKE INDEX

Date_____ Place_____ Hiked With_____

Distance_____ Duration_____ Conditions_____

Backpack ❏   Day Pack ❏   No Pack ❏

Prompt Pages Used_____

Extra Notes_____

_____

_____

HIKE INDEX

Date_____ Place_____ Hiked With_____

Distance_____ Duration_____ Conditions_____

Backpack ❏   Day Pack ❏   No Pack ❏

Prompt Pages Used_____

Extra Notes_____

_____

_____

HIKE INDEX

Date_____ Place_____ Hiked With_____

Distance_____ Duration_____ Conditions_____

Backpack ❏   Day Pack ❏   No Pack ❏

Prompt Pages Used_____

Extra Notes_____

_____

_____

Author's Note

Hiking, backpacking, and camping of any kind do amazing things for my state of mind and well-being, but doing those things alone is different. When I'm out there, often with no one for miles, something subtle shifts in how I think, how I plan, and even how I act. Out there alone, there's only the here and now. Yes, it can be scary, but if you push past that, it can turn into exhilaration. When I hike alone, it's thrilling to realize I'm consistently functioning in the present moment—which is unlike me! Often things are reduced to putting one foot in front of the other, itself a type of meditation, and listening to nature and becoming a part of the massive wild world around me, instead of tuning it out as I might do with other hikers present. It's also interesting to discover where my thoughts go when I break or set up camp for the night.

There have been times when I wished I could have shared a stunning view, a triumph, or a beautiful moment with someone, and there have been times when I wish I'd had this very journal to keep me company, to capture fleeting feelings and thoughts and insights in its pages. Revisiting those times and reliving some of the most peaceful and profound experiences on the trail makes me happy. I hope you found this journal useful, informative, and most importantly, a companion to you on your journey.

Here's to many more trails in the future!

—Jennifer Doehring

About the Author

JENNIFER DOEHRING is an artist and illustrator living in Southern California. When she's not creating art or writing funny stories for kids, she's out in nature, traveling the world, and backpacking in as many national parks as possible.